HELENA CITRÓNOVÁ

HELENA CITRÓNOVÁ
libretto by S.P. Somtow
@ 2018 Somtow Sucharitkul

published by
Diplodocus Press
Los Angeles • Bangkok

ISBN: 978-1-940999-1-97

First Edition

0 9 8 7 6 5 4 3 2 1

HELENA CITRÓNOVÁ

an opera in eleven scenes
by Somtow Sucharitkul

libretto by S.P. Somtow

from the life of Helena Citrónová

Diplodocus Press
Los Angeles • Bangkok

Characters

Helena Citrónová,	soprano
Zdenka, her friend	soprano
Rožinka, her sister	mezzo-soprano
Franz Wunsch, an SS officer	baritone
Oskar, an SS officer	bass
Janek, a kapo	baritone
Interrogator	bass
Captain	baritone

Chorus:	prisoners
	SS-guards

Instrumentation

Piccolo
2 Flutes
Alto Flute
2 Oboes
Cor Anglais
E flat clarinet
2 Clarinets
Bass Clarinet
2 Bassoons
Contrabassoon

4 Horns
3 Trumpets
3 Trombones
Tuba

Harp
3 Percussionists
Timpani

Piano
Celesta
Organ

Strings

BANDA:

Viola, clarinet, percussion, out-of-tune piano

my only love, sprung from my only hate!

Romeo and Juliet

der Tod ist ein Meister aus Deutschland
sein Auge ist blau
er trifft dich mit bleierner Kugel
er trifft dich genau

Paul Celan

HELENA CITRÓNOVÁ

an opera in eleven scenes

ACT ONE

ONE: SELECTION

A train station, before dawn. A prelude plays, ominous and anguished. Guards patrol.

Suddenly a whistle blows. Frantic activity. The sound of a train pulling in just off-stage. Jewish prisoners are being herded onto the platform. A banda plays welcoming music, jaunty but listless.

GUARDS
Faster!   Faster! Women and children
to the right!
Men to the left!
Move it! Faster!

PRISONERS
Where are we? What is this place?
I'm hungry! I'm frightened *(etc. etc.)*

Men, women and children stand huddled and confused, muttering.

GUARDS
Leave your baggage! It will be
returned to you.
Faster! Faster! Take nothing!
Nothing!

Baggage is being piled up and taken away by prisoners.

GUARDS
Not fast enough!

The guards beginning beating the prisoners.

*A doctor in a lab coat moves back and forth, pointing
people out. Among the guards with him is Franz Wunsch
and a fellow SS-man, Oskar. The prisoners are being
selected ... some for immediate death, others for work.*

FRANZ
You, you, and you. Over there.

OLD MAN
But that's the queue for the dead.

FRANZ
Dead now, dead later, what does it matter?

OLD MAN
But they said we could work.

FRANZ
Not you, old man.

OLD MAN
But sir — I assure you — I can work.

Franz shoots him. He crumples to the platform.

FRANZ
Not any more.

Among the new arrivals, a woman has been watching Franz. This is Helena Citronova. She turns away in horror.

OSKAR
That's a likely one. Shall I
save her for you, Franz?

FRANZ
No, thank you, Oskar. I've already eaten.

OSKAR
Why not? To have these creatures —
It is of no more account
than a ewe to a shepherd
on a cold night.
But you have scruples, my friend.
You are still young.
I'll show you what to do.
          (to Helena)
Do you have a name, woman?

HELENA
Helena Citrónová.

Oskar slaps Helena resoundingly.

                    OSKAR
          Bitch! Wrong answer!
          There are no names for Jews,
          only numbers. Go!

*He prods her with a rifle butt, and the women move
toward the barracks.*

                    OSKAR
          You must never forget, Franz,
          that they're not really people.
          They are the dark past,
          the primordial slime.

                    FRANZ
          No. I won't forget, sir.

                 INTERMEZZO

TWO: HATE

Dead of night. Helena climbs over sleeping woman to reach the toilet pail. Zdenka, a young prisoner, is trying to reach the pail as well.

ZDENKA
(pushing)
Get off! I got here first.

HELENA
You could be more polite. I only want to pee.

ZDENKA
Polite? You think this is the Hotel Sacher?
(she squats over the bucket.)

HELENA
What is this place? Why are we here?

ZDENKA
Don't ask such things. There are no answers.
This is a place where they kill you.
That is all.

HELENA
But what if one wanted to live?

ZDENKA
Is that what you want?

HELENA
Yes.

ZDENKA
Then listen, for though I may not
look like much,
here in this topsy-turvy world
perhaps I am your guardian angel.
Tomorrow, come with me.

HELENA
Why would you want to help me?

ZDENKA
Because you spoke of politeness,
and reminded me
that another world exists.
I am Zdenka.

HELENA
Helena Citrónová.

ZDENKA
Helena, let's promise each other
To live if we can,
though our only sustenance
be hate.

HELENA
Hate? Shall hate keep me alive?
Then I will hate
as I've never hated.

ZDENKA
Yes. Hate should be your guide —

HELENA
My shield. My armor.

ZDENKA
Your protection. Your god.

HELENA
Let's empty our souls
of all we knew before
and fill them again with hate.

ZDENKA
Hate, hate.

Weeping, the two women cling to each other in the
darkness.

INTERMEZZO

THREE: CANADA

Seated women are opening luggage and sorting through piles of clothes. Helena Citronova comes in, accompanied by Zdenka, a young woman. There is a battered out of tune piano in one corner of the room. A lockbox stands on a table in the center of the room. Through the window, there can be seen a view of the crematorium, and the chimneys through which dark smoke occasionally belches.

WOMEN
Canada, Canada,
Land of milk and honey,
Canada, Canada,
with rivers of gold.

ZDENKA
Quick. Put these on.

HELENA
Whose are they?

ZDENKA
You don't want to know. That person is gone. Up the chimney. Put on these.

They will save your life.

Helena puts on the uniform quickly.

> ZDENKA
> Here we sort out the belongings of the dead.
> Quick. Sit. Sort.
> Look. Here ... a diamond, rolled up
> in an old sock. We put these things in
> the lockbox. Over there.

> HELENA
> I've found an apple.

> ZDENKA
> Eat it quickly. No time for regrets.

Helena finds cash.

> HELENA
> Look. There's money.

> ZDENKA
> Take it to the lockbox.
> Keep your eyes downcast
> at all times.

Helena takes the money to the lockbox. Janek, a Kapo, has seen her.

> JANEK
> You — you don't look right.

Helena keeps her eyes downcast.

JANEK
You don't belong here.

Helena turns to Zdenka, who immediately ignores her.

JANEK
As soon as the day is over, you will
report to the punishment block.

He turns away. Helena returns to her post.

ZDENKA
Oh, God. He has sentenced you to death.

HELENA
I'm not afraid.
I will have a roof over my head tonight,
and the gift you have me,
hate, for company.

WOMEN
Canada, Canada,
Land of milk and honey,
with streets of pure gold.
Canada, Canada,
Land without chimneys,
Belching forth memories
Where ovens bring bread
Not death, not death.

SS-MEN
(off-stage)
Hoch soll er leben,
Hoch soll er leben,
Dreimal hoch!

Oskar, Franz, and other SS-men enter the area. All the
women immediately stand, heads bowed.

OSKAR
Attention, you bitches!
One of you is going to be blessed today.
Today is the birthday of
our comrade, Franz.
Surely there is one among you
able to sing?

JANEK
Oh, all can sing, sir.
Take your pick.

OSKAR
But Franz wants to hear
the music of his homeland.
He's sick, the poor boy,
Sick of your music.

JANEK
(to Helena)
Hey, you!
You were brazen enough
To barge into Canada.

Let's hear you sing yourself
out of the hangman's noose.
>   *(to Oskar)*
Sir, she disguised herself
to work here,
so I sentenced her to the punishment cell.

OSKAR

Good work.
>   *(to Helena)*
Give us a German song.

HELENA

I know no German songs, sir.

OSKAR
>   *(striking her)*
Vermin.

One of the SS-officers sits at the piano and begins to play Schubert.

OSKAR

They know nothing of culture.

But Helena does know this song, and in a faltering voice begins to sing "An die Musik."

HELENA

Du holde Kunst, in wieviel grauen Stunden
Wo mich des Lebens wilder Kreis umstrickt
Hast du mein Herz zur warmer Lieb
>   *entzunden*

Hast mich in eine beßre Welt entrückt.

*Franz is transfixed. The pianist stops playing, laughs.
The women giggle nervously. Oskar and Janek are
confused.*

FRANZ
Please. Go on.

After a bit of hesitation, the pianist continues.

HELENA
Oft hat ein Seufzer, deiner Harf' entflossen,
Ein süßer, heiliger Akkord von dir
Den Himmel beßrer Zeiten mir erschlossen,
   Du holde Kunst, ich danke dir dafür!

*The other performers seem to recede into darkness.
Helena and Franz appear alone, illuminated by some eerie
inner light.*

FRANZ
You know our language,
Helena Citrónová.

HELENA
No! Don't say my name.
We have no names here, only numbers.

FRANZ
It need not be so.

HELENA

Oh yes. It must be so,
Lest this mad universe
you have created
fall apart.

FRANZ

I will not have it so.

HELENA

Oh, but you must.
We both have roles to play.

FRANZ

But what of choice?
And what of self-determination?

HELENA

Play your role,
young officer.
Do you not know your lines?
Next, you must send me to my death.

FRANZ

No, I —

The spell is broken as the SS-men begin singing the birthday song again.

SS-MEN

Hoch soll er leben,
Hoch soll er leben,
Dreimal hoch!

And they are gone. Canada is plunged in gloom.

JANEK
Back to work!

WOMEN
Canada, Canada,
Land of milk and honey,
Canada, Canada,
with rivers of gold.

ZDENKA
You're looking at him.

HELENA
He doesn't seem like the others.

ZDENKA
He is.

HELENA
How can you know?

ZDENKA
Helena, I am wise beyond my years,
I've been here for months
and I'm still alive.
What's in your eyes,
I've seen it.

It's dangerous. It will kill you.
What's in your eyes
is hope.

HELENA

What's wrong with hope?

ZDENKA

Hope is forbidden.
Hope will kill you
faster than the gas.
Kill the hope now,
Kill it before it kills you.
Remember what I've taught you.
Hate. Hate.

HELENA

Yes. I will remember.
Hate. Hate.

INTERMEZZO

FOUR: LOVE

It is a few days later in Canada.   A front-room area is the office of Franz Wunsch. Helena, Zdenka, and other women are working as usual. Janek is pacing up and down.

> WOMEN
>> Canada, Canada,
>> Land of milk and honey,
>> with streets of pure gold.
>> Canada, Canada,
>> Land without chimneys,
>> Belching forth memories
>> Where ovens bring bread
>> Not death, not death.

Abruptly, Franz enters and all the women stand up, looking down at the floor. He walks past where Helena has been working. He stops for a moment. Then, as though by accident, he lets a folded note fall to her feet.

Then he walks away and the women return to work.

Helena picks up the note and gives it a cursory glance. Then she carefully crumples it up and, when no one is looking, she swallows it.

ZDENKA
Why did you swallow it?
What did it say?

HELENA
I only caught a few words
before I realized
it must be destroyed.

ZDENKA
What was it? A threat?
A demand for an assignation?

HELENA
Worse.
He said that he loves me.

ZDENKA
Then you did well.
Rape, violence, forcible violations
These are the realities here.
But love is not permitted.

HELENA
I know. I am learning.
I'd rather die than be with him.

JANEK
Citrónová!
Wunsch wants to see you.

HELENA
(to Zdenka)
He can see me.
He can beat me.
He can rape me.
The person inside
will be untouched.

She goes towards Wunsch's office. He motions her inside with the crook of his finger.

FRANZ
Do my nails.

HELENA
I'm not a manicurist.

FRANZ
Just do them. That way I can look at you.
Even for a minute.

HELENA
I remember the first time
I laid eyes on you —

FRANZ
The song. It was beautiful.

HELENA

No! On the platform.
You've already forgotten.
We are not names. We are numbers.

FRANZ

The platform!

HELENA

You killed an old man
because he wanted to work.

FRANZ

Yes, I kill. I am here to kill people.
It is my job.

HELENA

I can't look at you.
Don't bring me here.
Don't make me do your nails.
I'm leaving.

FRANZ

Even knowing that I could kill you?

*Wunsch pulls out a pistol. He forces her into a kneeling
position, puts the gun to her head.*

FRANZ

Try to leave now.
You won't make it
through the doorway.

Helena wrests herself free with a supreme effort.

> HELENA
>
> Then kill me.

> FRANZ
>
> You'd disobey me?
> You'd choose death over a manicure?

> HELENA
>
> At least the choice would be my own.

Dignified and unafraid, she walks out of Wunsch's room.

The women continue their work. Franz, alone, reflects on his confrontation with the defiant woman.

> FRANZ
>
> "At least the choice would be my own."
> With these words
> she dares what I cannot dare,
> does what I may not do.
>
> I was seventeen years old
> when I joined the SS.
> There are things I was taught,
> There are things I know
> Things I've always known.
> The jews are our enemies.
> They bled us dry,
> polluted our culture,
> destroyed our humanity.

I hate the jews.
They are not human.
I know these things.
They are my truth.

So what then
is Helena Citrónová?
She cannot be a jew,
she cannot be a number.
One doesn't love
a number.
One dare not love
a jew.
These are things I was taught,
These are things that I know.

So who then
is Helena Citrónová?
And by saying "who"
do I not admit
she is not a number?
that it is possible
she may be human?
that therefore all I do
may be inhuman?

These thoughts
may not be thought.
The choices
are not mine to make.
I must stay true
to what I know is true,
to the person I know I am.

So I must kill her.

But I know I will not,
And this knowledge
Tears me asunder.

INTERMEZZO

FIVE: CREMATORIUM

It is dusk, after curfew. Searchlights. A barking dog, and guards strolling. A group of prisoners is being herded into the crematorium with rifle blows and shouts.

GUARDS
Inside! Quickly!
The sooner you go in
The sooner you'll come out!

Helena rushes onto the stage.

HELENA
My sister!
Someone save her!
My sister and her children!

FIRST GUARD
You there! Curfew violation!

SECOND GUARD
Stop or I'll shoot!

HELENA

They have my sister!
They have her children!
Save her, save them!

The doors of the crematorium slam shut. Franz Wunsch comes running into the scene. He throws Helena to the ground and begins beating her savagely.

FRANZ

Quiet! Don't resist!

HELENA

Why should I?
You are all the same.

FRANZ

Quickly ... the sister's name ... quickly ...
If I don't beat you they will shoot you....

HELENA

Rožinka ...
and her two chidren ...

FRANZ

Don't speak of children!

HELENA

Rožinka and her small son
and her daughter —

FRANZ
Children can't live here.

*Franz throws Helena roughly down. She crawls after him
as he throws open the doors of the crematorium. A
terrible, deathly hubbub is heard. After a moment Franz
emerges, dragging Rožinka with him. She tries to get free,
to run back into the crematorium. The door slams shut.*

ROŽINKA
My children!

FRANZ
Don't think of them again.
They are happy.
They are safe.

*He throws Rožinka out into the yard. She falls, weak and
in pain. Helena crawls towards her.*

ROŽINKA
Helena ... they won't let me see my children ...

HELENA
Oh Rožinka, do not think of them.
You are alive.
For this moment, you are alive.

*Rožinka collapses. Helena and Franz sing, neither of
them daring to look at each other.*

HELENA
Is there are price for this?

FRANZ
No price. How could I exact a price?

HELENA
You've given a life.

FRANZ
It's not much of a life.
It's only a reprieve,
a stretching of the boundary.
She'll die another time,
when she falls foul of an SS-man,
when she fails to react swiftly enough.

HELENA
Still it is a life
and life for an hour or a day
in this place
comes with a price.

FRANZ
I don't bargain.
I'm not a jew.

HELENA
But unwittingly, you have already traded
your innocence.

FRANZ
Don't dare to question me!

HELENA

You've bargained away
Your terrible certainty
for something far more terrible
ambiguity and doubt.

FRANZ

Do not presume
To see through me
with your devious philosophy
and your godless logic.

HELENA

Knowing that death is close
Makes me see clearly.

FRANZ

You are not afraid.

HELENA

I am not afraid.

FRANZ

Death is always beside you.

HELENA

Death will come upon me
In a moment, in a breath.

FRANZ

Give me that moment,
Give me that breath,

For I would fill it to bursting
With what I am feeling.

HELENA

How can you dare to say
You love me,
In this place,
Knowing your place and mine?

FRANZ

I can dare
because you see me.
In the desolation
in the smoke
You see me.

HELENA

I see you.
I see a gift you gave me.
I see the price of that gift.
I do not yet say
That I can love you.

FRANZ

Then do not say it.

HELENA

I do not say I love you.

FRANZ

No. Do not say it.

HELENA
I will not say I love you.

FRANZ
But I will say it
for us both.
I will say *I love you*.

HELENA
No. Never say it. Never say
I love you.

Slowly, Helena and Franz turn towards each other.
Rožinka moans. Smoke fills the scene as the crematorium
begins its work. Helena does not look at Franz, but does
not try to stop him when he reaches out to touch her.

END OF ACT ONE

ACT TWO

SIX: NIGHT

Helena is alone, in a place beyond reach. She sings to herself.

HELENA

Love is the way
The way is death
If I go forward
Stilled is my breath
If I retreat
I fall to the ground
If I escape
I'll never be found
Love is the way
The way is death
O Franz, O Franz.

Darkness has fallen
Darkness has come
Darkness has rendered me
Deaf and dumb

Only in darkness
Shall this love thrive
In the darkness of death
We are truly alive
Love is the way
The way is death
O Franz, O Franz.

Love is the way
The way is death
I breathe in darkness
With every breath
For no ray of light
Can be allowed
To penetrate
This smoky shroud
O Franz, O Franz.

Darkness is dancing
In your eyes
You bring me a truth
That is woven from lies
Through the brick wall
Encased in steel hate
Yet yours is the one truth
I await.
Your name is love
Your name is death
I cry your name
with my last breath
O Franz, O Franz, O Franz.

SEVEN: CHIMNEY

Canada. Rožinka has come to work and sits beside her sister. The women sort the belongings and when they come upon a bit of food, they wolf it down furtively.

WOMEN
Canada, Canada,
Land of milk and honey,
with streets of pure gold.
Canada, Canada,
Land without chimneys,
Belching forth memories
Where ovens bring bread
Not death, not death.

ROŽINKA
Helena ... tell me about my children.

HELENA
Again, again, Rožinka?

ROŽINKA
I can never hear enough.
I dream about them every night.

HELENA
All right then.
On the other side of the barbed wire
there is a kindergarten.
The children there have plenty to eat
and never get whipped.

ROŽINKA
Never?

HELENA
No. The guards are very kind there.
They are more like nannies.   e
At night they tell the children stories.

ROŽINKA
Oh, oh ... do you think we can visit them?

HELENA
Very very rarely ... on very special days.

ROŽINKA
Oh, oh ... I'll live for that special day.

ZDENKA
Do her a kindness, Helena!

Spare her the hope!

ROŽINKA
What is she saying?

ZDENKA
You enter through the door,
You exit through the chimney.

ROŽINKA
No!
Those are tales
told to frighten us
tales of demons
fables told to children!

HELENA
Zdenka! Don't!

*Zdenka drags Rožinka to the window. Smoke is pouring
from the chimney.*

ZDENKA
You can see them on very special days?
Wrong, Rožinka.
You can see them every day.
Every day in the smoke.
That's where your children live.

Rožinka screams and moans.

HELENA
Why so heartless, Zdenka?

Aren't *they* evil enough already?

ZDENKA
How would you know?
You're in love with one of *them!*

WOMEN
Helena the whore!
Helena gets to live,
Her sister is dragged
from the chamber of death
... and where are *our* sisters?

FIRST WOMAN
Up the chimney.

SECOND WOMAN
Our mothers, our fathers ...
FIRST WOMAN
Our children, our friends ...

WOMEN
All gone up the chimney ...
and soon it's our turn ...
But not Helena,
Not Helena the whore.

HELENA
I never said I loved him!

Franz Wunsch stands the doorway. All the women fall silent, their eyes downcast. Only Helena, defiant, looks him in the eye.

FRANZ
No. She never said she loved me.

Rožinka hugs herself, rocks back and forth.

FRANZ
Never say it, Helena.

HELENA
I will not.

They look at each other as the music swells to an:

INTERMEZZO

EIGHT: SECRETS

In front of the crematorium. Prisoners are being herded in the background. Among the guards is Franz. Crossing the line of inmates being moved to the crematorium is another line, returning in single file from some activity. Among the returning prisoners are Helena, Rožinka and Zdenka. The lines move slowly enough for Franz and Helena to have a brief conversation.

> HELENA
> No, no, not now, it's too dangerous.

> FRANZ
> Later, then.

> HELENA
> Later.

Eyes downcast she continues to walk.

FIRST WOMAN

Traitor!

SECOND WOMAN

Whore!

WOMEN
(whispering)
Whore, whore,
sleeping with the enemy
while we suffer.

GUARD

Be quiet!

FIRST WOMAN

She's not so attractive,
the bitch.
Why, if Wunsch had seen me first —

SECOND WOMAN

I'd be warming him up
and getting fat.

GUARD

Silence!

*Some of the women are beaten, causing the line to stall
and making it possible for Franz and Helena to stay in the
same spot for a moment to prolong their conversation.*

FRANZ

When can we speak again?

HELENA
Why? Every moment we are talking now
is snatched from another's pain.

FRANZ
In my office, then, tomorrow.
I'll summon you
under pretext of punishment.

OSKAR
(to Helena)
Why do speak to this SS-man?
Why are your eyes not lowered to the
ground?
(slaps her)

Helena raises her eyes once more.

FRANZ
Look at the ground Helena.
Do not look at me.
I love you.

OSKAR
Move along, bitches!
The beating is over.

FRANZ
No! Do not say it!
Look away.

One line of prisoners has entered the crematorium and the doors are being slammed shut. The line of women of which Rožinka, Helena and the others form a part is exiting in the opposite direction. Oskar and Franz remain.

OSKAR

There is something about
the way that one looks at you.

FRANZ

Which one?

OSKAR

The impertinent one. The one
I had to slap.

FRANZ

Oh. Her. She works under me
in Canada. I was just ...
giving her extra instructions.

OSKAR

No ... there is something hidden ...
there is a secret.

FRANZ

You imagine too much.

OSKAR

You're a bad liar, Franz.

He signals. Two guards appear with Janek. They drag Helena out of the queue.

JANEK
Send her to Block 11.

HELENA
I've done nothing!

ARRESTING GUARD
Prisoner: you are being detained
on suspicion of having illicit carnal relations
with a member of a superior race.

WOMEN
Block 11!
That is like a death sentence.
Who has told the authorities?
It wasn't me. It wasn't me.
It was you! Oh, no, I'm not a rat.
Rat! Rat!

OSKAR
Ha! Franz! You are moved!
You are visibly moved!
It is evidence!

FRANZ
Heil Hitler!
I am not, sir!

Resolutely, he looks away.

> OSKAR
> (summoning more guards)
> Wunsch: it is my duty to inform you
> That you are under arrest
> for the crime of racial pollution.

Franz looks at Helena, who looks away.

> FRANZ

It's an outrage!

> OSKAR

I'm sorry, Franz,
but your eyes betray you.

*The guards take hold of Franz and start to drag him away.
From across the stage, the two lovers look at each other
clearly for the first time. Then they are taken away in
opposite directions.*

> OSKAR
There are no secrets here.

> ZDENKA
There are no secrets here.

*Oskar and Zdenka look at each other enigmatically as the
music sweeps us into an*

INTERMEZZO

NINE: TORTURE

The stage is divided into two. On one side, a filthy, claustrophobic cell in which Helena has been restrained. On the other, a brightly lit interrogation chamber. Between the two rooms, concrete walls and a narrow passageway. In the interrogation chamber, Franz is sitting, very straight, across a table from a SS officer in the uniform of a captain.

CAPTAIN
You have known this jewess for ...

FRANZ
A few weeks, Herr Hauptsturmfürhrer.

CAPTAIN
And when did you have carnal knowledge of her?

FRANZ
I haven't, Herr Hauptsturmführer.

CAPTAIN
(slamming the table)
Liar!

The door to Helena's cell opens and an interrogator enters
accompanied by two guards.

INTERROGATOR
Wake her!

The guards slap Helena awake.

INTERROGATOR
No sleep! Who said you could sleep?
Stinking jew whore.

HELENA
I've told you everything I know.

INTERROGATOR
No you haven't.
What did you hope to gain
by seducing your betters?
You're going to die anyway.

HELENA
I have done nothing.

At the same time, the interrogation of Franz continues.

CAPTAIN
Don't think they're not tempting,
Subhuman though they may be.

Don't think I blame you.
They're enticing, they're wicked,
They'll do anything for a crust,
or a night without a beating.

FRANZ
I won't confess to what I haven't done.

CAPTAIN
Just sign the thing.
You'll get a slap on the wrist.

*Back to Helena's interrogation. She is being savagely
beaten. She screams.*

INTERROGATOR
Slut! Bitch! Whore! Jewess sow!

HELENA
I'm innocent, I'm innocent.

FRANZ
What slap on the wrist?

CAPTAIN
Nothing. Perhaps a demotion,
a few benefits withdrawn.

FRANZ
For that, I will not lie.
I am innocent.

HELENA
I am guilty of nothing
Except a glance,
a word.

INTERROGATOR
A glance! A word!
Beat her!

HELENA
(screams)

INTERROGATOR
Confess!

FRANZ
What is the sound,
that bloodcurdling sound?

CAPTAIN
You know too well.
Here is the confession.
Sign it.
I will be back.

The captain leaves the room.

GUARD
She's fainted, sir.

INTERROGATOR
Leave her awhile.
At some stage

she will eventually confess;
they all do.
Then hang her.

GUARD

And if she doesn't confess?

INTERROGATOR

Throw her back.

The interrogator and the guards leave the room.
Separated by walls, the voices of Helena and Franz meld
into a tormented love duet.

HELENA

They ask me to confess
to a sordid act
a business arrangement
the confession of a whore.
They do not ask me to confess
to love.

FRANZ

They ask me to confess
to a transaction,
to carnal knowledge,
to a bestial perversion.
They do not ask me to confess
to love.

HELENA

And yet
Perhaps I dare confess it

to myself ...

FRANZ

And yet
I dared confess my love
to her...

HELENA

Because I have endured such pain ...

FRANZ

Because she has endured such pain ...

HELENA

I will keep silent still

FRANZ

I will keep silent still

HELENA

I won't confess

FRANZ

I won't confess

HELENA

I'll take his image to the showers
Into the gas
and up the chimney
and down to the huddled grave
where they pile us up
what pieces remain
his name will lie

among the ashes

FRANZ

When this all ends
I'll take her with me
it can't be long now
till the end comes
If only I can keep her
clinging to this thread
if only I can keep the door ajar
till we can find
a new beginning

HELENA

No no it can't be long now
each day I stare
at the blackened sky
and know my end
and know there is no beginning
here there is only ending
only ending

FRANZ

I will say it to the emptiness
Helena Citrónová
I love you

HELENA

Even in my aloneness I dare not say it
Franz Wunsch
I love you

The music crescendoes as, worn out, the lovers fall asleep each one alone and isolated even from the reality of the concentration camp ... and the orchestra swells to an

INTERMEZZO

TEN: DEATH MARCH

*Distant bombs and sirens. The prisoners are being herded
out of the barracks. It is snowing. Women are being
turned out into the cold, barely clad, without real shoes.
Guards are shouting at them.*

> GUARDS
>
> Quick! Quick!
> You must get to the next encampment
> ahead of the Russians.

> OSKAR
>
> Anyone who dawdles will be shot.

Rožinka, Helena, and Zdenka are among the women.

> GUARD
>
> Answer to your names!
> Applebaum!

FIRST WOMAN

Yes!

GUARD

Abramowicz!
Alzheimer!

SECOND WOMAN

She's dead, sir!

GUARD

Then bring out the corpse!
The count must be correct!

They begin herding them off in small clusters. Zdenka appeals to Oskar.

ZDENKA

Please, sir — can I have something for my
feet —

I'm so tired — the frostbite will gnaw off my
toes —

Consider what I let you do —

Oskar shoots her.

OSKAR

Animal.

Zdenka falls to the ground and her body is kicked off-stage. Franz appears. In full view of the others, he hands a thick sweater to Helena and a shawl to Rožinka.

HELENA
Don't do these things. They'll see you.

OSKAR
What are you doing?
Haven't you learned your lesson?

FRANZ
You fool, Oskar!
It doesn't matter anymore.
You think you're just retreating
to a safe haven
and you'll build more factories
and work these jews to death —
It's over, Oskar.

OSKAR
Not until it's over, Franz.

HELENA
Leave the things and go!
You're risking your life.

FRANZ
Take this. It's a note.
This will end soon.
You have nowhere to go.
Your home is destroyed,
or given to others.
Your wealth has been seized
and spent.
This is my mother's address.

She will look after you.

HELENA
Why, Franz, why?

FRANZ
Don't ask such things.
What has happened between us
is a mystery.

Whistles are blowing. The prisoners are being beaten into line.

FRANZ
Goodbye.
Don't look at me.

He walks away. She hesitates ... turns her downcast eyes upward to see him clearly for the first time. He looks back.

FRANZ
No! Don't look!

He goes to her and slaps her resoundingly.

FRANZ
Don't look at me again!

The line of prisoners moves off.

INTERMEZZO

ELEVEN: HOME

*Many months later. In front of Franz's house in Vienna ...
an apartment in a townhouse in a nondescript street. The
stage is divided exactly as it was during the interrogation
scene, but one side shows the interior of the Wunsch
household. Frau Wunsch is sitting in front of a fireplace;
Franz is stoking the fire.*

FRAU WUNSCH
Listen! Someone outside.

FRANZ
Surely not, mother.
It's late.

FRAU WUNSCH
They could come for you
at any hour.

My son, the war criminal!
When you left this house
at seventeen
in your shiny uniform
I never dreamed
we would be waiting here
on a cold winter's night
for the police to come.

FRANZ

I'm sure it is no one, mother.
But I'll go see.

FRAU WUNSCH

Turn on the light.

Outside the house, Helena has come down the street. She is holding the note Franz gave her. When the light in the window comes on, she approaches the door and puts her hand on the doorbell. But she hesitates.

FRANZ

Helena Citrónová.

FRAU WUNSCH

What did you say?

HELENA

Should I ring the doorbell?
Should I fulfill the unspoken promise
Should I bring the nightmare to an end?

FRANZ

Will she enter?
Will she forgive?
Will she fulfill the unspoken promise
and bring my nightmares to an end?

HELENA

My father told me once
Don't ever forget
you're a jew.
And how could I forget,
knowing that it was being a jew
that sent me to that place
that killed him,
my mother, my sister's children ...
then, when the war was over
for the others
scurrying under tables
for fear of the Russians,
hiding in basements,
eating from rubbish dumps?

FRANZ

Can she ever understand
that I too was a prisoner
and that she was for me
the one redeeming truth?

HELENA

Can I enter?
Can I forgive?

FRANZ

Should I run down
and throw the door open?
Should I embrace her
Kiss her
Show her the hidden love
I could not show before?

HELENA

No, Franz, no.
I dare not forget the nightmare
Because I dare not forget
who I am,
To end the nightmare
Will make the nightmare real.
Let our love stay hidden.

FRANZ

She is turning away.
Oh Helena,
Stay, Helena, stay.

HELENA

I must turn away.
To ring the doorbell
is to deny my nature.
Yes, Franz, I loved you,
but that is past
and the past does not redeem us
It chains us
It suffocates us
but the past kills love
as surely as the poison gas

and the black smoke
of annihilation.

FRANZ

Stay, Helena ...
because in you
I was redeemed ...
You showed me how
to cast off the chains
and to breathe
a different air,
an air of purity,
amid the poison gas
and the black smoke
of annihilation.

HELENA
(to herself)
Oh Franz, I cannot stay.
I cannot ring the bell.
What would I say to you?

FRAU WUNSCH

Who is it, Franz?
Are you talking to yourself?

FRANZ

There is no one there, mother
I was just thinking
about someone I used to know.

HELENA
(to herself)
Goodbye, Franz.

FRANZ
(to himself)
Goodbye, Helena.

He switches off the light. Helena walks away slowly.
Night and fog subsume the stage.

END OF THE OPERA

AFTERWORD

For the last five years I have been working on this opera, *Helena Citrónová*. I cannot get the subject out of my mind. The true story of a Slovak Jew in Auschwitz who had a passionate and searing relationship with an SS-man has so many things to tell us today. It asks questions that make us question all that makes us human.

Questions like: What is love, in the end? And, Can love possibly exist in a situation as extreme as Auschwitz?

The lesson I have learned from this story is that in the end, the Holocaust was not only about telling someone they should starve, that they should be tortured, that they should be worked to death, that they should be gassed and cremated. It was really about telling someone, "You are not a person."

If your life's work consists of telling people, day in, day out, "You are not a person," then in the end it will happen to you too. You, who steal humanity from your victims, must inevitably lose your own humanity.

This then is a story about a woman who, though trapped in the darkest of possible hells, would not give up her personhood.

It is the story of a man who should have given up his personhood, but instead found redemption in this woman's refusal, redemption in the very thing that he had been taught not to regard as a person.

I was born a few years after the Second World War ended, in a place far from the events of this opera. But several times in my life I have had vivid dreams about Auschwitz. Since I saw an interview with Helena on a BBC documentary, she has haunted me.

— S.P. Somtow

ABOUT THE AUTHOR

Once referred to by the *In-ternational Herald Tribune* as "the most well-known expatriate Thai in the world," Somtow Sucharitkul is no longer an expatriate, since he has returned to Thailand after five decades of wandering the world. He is best known as an award-winning novelist and a composer of operas.

Born in Bangkok, Somtow grew up in Europe and was educated at Eton and Cambridge. His first career was in music and in the 1970s he acquired a reputation as a revolutionary com-poser, the first to combine Thai and Western instruments in radical new sonorities. Conditions in the arts in the region at the time proved so traumatic for the young composer that he suffered a major burnout, emigrated to the United States, and reinvented himself as a novelist.

His earliest novels were in the science fiction field but he soon began to cross into other genres. In his 1984 novel Vampire Junction, he injected a new literary inventiveness into the horror genre, in the words of Robert Bloch, author of Psycho, "skillfully combining the styles of Stephen King, William Burroughs, and the author of the Revelation to John." *Vampire Junction* was voted one of the forty all-time greatest horror books by the Horror Writers' Association, joining established classics like *Frankenstein* and *Dracula*.

In the 1990s Somtow became increasingly identified as a uniquely Asian writer with novels such as the semi-autobiographical *Jasmine Nights*. He won the World Fantasy Award, the highest accolade given in the world of fantastic literature, for his novella *The Bird Catcher*. His fifty-three books have sold about two million copies world-wide.

After becoming a Buddhist monk for a period in 2001, Somtow decided to refocus his attention on the country of his birth, founding Bangkok's first international opera company and returning to music, where he again reinvented himself, this time as a neo-Asian neo-Romantic composer. The Norwegian government commissioned his song cycle *Songs Before Dawn* for the 100th Anniversary of the Nobel Peace Prize, and he composed at the request of the government of Thailand his *Requiem: In Memoriam 9/11* which was dedicated to the victims of the 9/11 tragedy.

According to London's Opera magazine, "in just five years, Somtow has made Bangkok into the operatic hub of Southeast Asia." His operas on Thai themes, *Madana, Mae Naak,* and *Ayodhya,* have been well received by international critics. His most recent opera, *The Silent Prince,* was premiered in 2010 in Houston, and a fifth opera, *Dan no Ura,* premiered in Thailand in the 2013 season. Since then, he has composed five more operas, and is embarking on a ten opera cycle, *DasJati - Ten Lives of the Buddha,* which if completed will be the "biggest" single work in the history of performing arts.

He is increasingly in demand as a conductor specializing in opera and in the late-romantic composers like Mahler. His repertoire runs the entire gamut from Monteverdi to Wagner. His work has been especially lauded for its stylistic authenticity and its lyricism. The orchestra he founded in Bangkok, the Siam Philharmonic, has mounted the first complete Mahler cycle in the region.

He is the first recipient of Thailand's "Distinguished Silpathorn" award, given for an artist who has made and continues to make a major impact on the region's culture, from Thailand's Ministry of Culture.

BOOKS BY S.P. SOMTOW

General Fiction
The Shattered Horse
Jasmine Nights
Forgetting Places
The Other City of Angels (Bluebeard's Castle)
The Stone Buddha's Tears

Dark Fantasy
The Timmy Valentine Series:
  Vampire Junction
  Valentine
  Vanitas
Vampire Junction Special Edition
Moon Dance
Darker Angels
The Vampire's Beautiful Daughter

Science Fiction
Starship & Haiku
Mallworld
The Ultimate Mallworld
The Ultimate, Ultimate, Ultimate Mallworld
Chronicles of the High Inquest:
  Light on the Sound
  The Darkling Wind
  The Throne of Madness
  Utopia Hunters

Chroniques de l'Inquisition - Volume 1 (omnibus)
Chroniques de l'Inquisition - Volume 2 (omnibus)

The Aquiliad Series:
  Aquila in the New World
  Aquila and the Iron Horse
  Aquila and the Sphinx

Fantasy
The Riverrun Trilogy:
  Riverrun
  Armorica
  Yestern
The Riverrun Trilogy (omnibus)
The Fallen Country
Wizard's Apprentice
The Snow Dragon (omnibus)

Media Tie-in
The Alien Swordmaster
Symphony of Terror
The Crow - Temple of Night
Star Trek: Do Comets Dream?

Chapbooks
Fiddling for Waterbuffaloes
I Wake from a Dream of a Drowned Star City
A Lap Dance with the Lobster Lady
Compassion — Two Perspectives
The Bird Catcher

Libretti
Mae Naak
Ayodhya
Madana
The Silent Prince
Dan no Ura
Helena Citronova
The Snow Dragon
Sama - The Faithful Son
Nemiraj - The Chariot of Heaven
Mahosadha - The Architect of Dreams
Chui Chai

Collections
My Cold Mad Father (in press)
Fire from the Wine Dark Sea
Chui Chai (Thai)
Nova (Thai)
The Pavilion of Frozen Women
Dragon's Fin Soup
Tagging the Moon
Face of Death (Thai)
Other Edens
S.P. Somtow's The Great Tales (Thai)
Terror Nova (in press)
Terror Antiqua (in press)

Essays, Poetry and Miscellanies
Opus Fifty
A Certain Slant of "I" (in press)

Sonnets about Serial Killers
Opera East
Victory in Vienna (ed.)
Three Continents (ed.)
Nirvana Express
Caravaggio x 2
The Maestro's Noctuary